SO-AYZ-182

CLASSICS
Illustrated®

Joseph Conrad
LORD JIM

essay by
John Barnes Ph.D.
Western State College

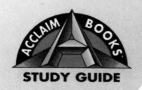

ACCLAIM BOOKS
STUDY GUIDE

CLASSICS
Illustrated ®

Lord Jim
Originally published as Classics Illustrated no. 139

Art by George Evans
Cover by Dennis Calero

For Classics Illustrated Study Guides
computer recoloring by VanHook Studios
editor: Madeleine Robins
assistant editor: Gregg Sanderson
design: Scott Friedlander

Classics Illustrated: Lord Jim © Twin Circle Publishing Co.,
a division of Frawley Enterprises; licensed to First Classics, Inc.
All new material and compilation © 1997 by Acclaim Books, Inc.

Dale-Chall R.L.: 6.85

ISBN 1-57840-066-X

Classics Illustrated® is a registered trademark of the Frawley Corporation.

Acclaim Books, New York, NY
Printed in the United States

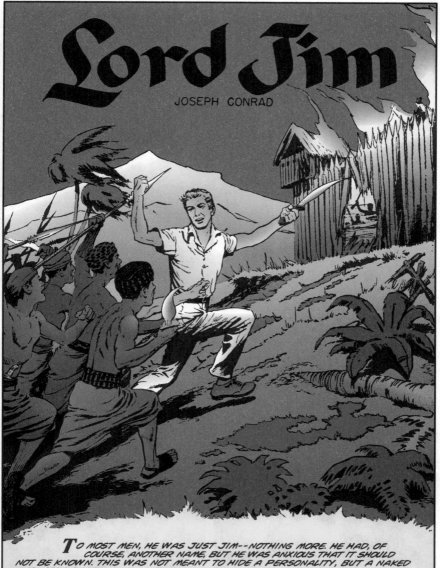

Lord Jim

JOSEPH CONRAD

To MOST MEN, HE WAS JUST JIM--NOTHING MORE. HE HAD, OF COURSE, ANOTHER NAME, BUT HE WAS ANXIOUS THAT IT SHOULD NOT BE KNOWN. THIS WAS NOT MEANT TO HIDE A PERSONALITY, BUT A NAKED AND UGLY FACT.

WHENEVER THE FACT BROKE THROUGH, JIM WOULD LEAVE THE SEAPORT WHERE HE HAPPENED TO BE, AND GO TO ANOTHER. AND THE FACT FOLLOWED HIM CASUALLY BUT INEVITABLY.

AFTERWARD, THE MALAYS OF THE JUNGLE VILLAGE WHERE HE ELECTED TO CONCEAL HIMSELF ADDED A WORD TO HIS NAME. THEY CALLED HIM TUAN JIM: AS ONE MIGHT SAY--LORD JIM.

ORIGINALLY, JIM CAME FROM A PARSONAGE IN ENGLAND. WHEN HIS VOCATION FOR THE SEA DECLARED ITSELF, HE WAS SENT TO A TRAINING SHIP FOR OFFICERS OF THE MERCANTILE MARINE.

HAVING A STEADY HEAD, HIS STATION WAS IN THE FORE-TOP OF THE SHIP. ALOFT, HE FELT HIMSELF A MAN DESTINED TO SHINE IN THE MIDST OF DANGER.

HE SAW HIMSELF SAVING PEOPLE FROM SINKING SHIPS.

HE QUELLED MUTINIES ON THE HIGH SEAS.

IN SHORT, HE DREAMED OF A LIFE OF STIRRING ADVENTURE, AND SAW HIMSELF AS AN EXAMPLE OF DEVOTION TO DUTY, AND AS UNFLINCHING AS A HERO IN A BOOK.

AFTER TWO YEARS OF TRAINING, JIM WENT TO SEA. HE MADE MANY VOYAGES, AND WHILE YET YOUNG, BECAME CHIEF MATE OF A FINE SHIP.

ONLY ONCE HAD HE A GLIMPSE OF THE MALICE THAT NOW AND THEN SHOWS ITSELF IN AN ANGRY SEA.

MAN! IT WILL BE A MIRACLE IF SHE LIVES THROUGH THIS GALE!

THE SHIP SURVIVED. BUT JIM, DISABLED BY A FALLING SPAR, WAS HOSPITALIZED IN AN EASTERN PORT. BY THE TIME HE RECOVERED, HIS SHIP HAD GONE.

AS SOON AS HE COULD WALK WITHOUT A STICK, HE BEGAN TO LOOK FOR A BERTH ON ANOTHER SHIP. ONE DAY . . .

'TIS THE PATNA. SHE'S OLD AS THE HILLS AND EATEN UP WITH RUST WORSE THAN A CONDEMNED WATER TANK.

SHE'S TAKING A LOAD OF PILGRIMS TO ONE OF THEIR HOLY CITIES. I HEAR SHE NEEDS A CHIEF MATE FOR THE RUN.

JIM SIGNED AS CHIEF MATE OF THE PATNA. WITH THE PILGRIMS PRAYING ON THE DECK, THE STEAMER CAST OFF AND BACKED AWAY FROM THE WHARF.

BESIDES JIM, THERE WERE FOUR WHITE MEN ON THE PATNA. THERE WAS THE CAPTAIN, WHO WAS THE KIND OF MAN WHO BULLIED EVERYONE HE WAS NOT AFRAID OF.

LOOK AT THOSE CATTLE.

AND THERE WERE THREE ENGINEERS.

HOW ABOUT GIVING ME A NIP, CHIEF?

ONLY ONE, MIND YOU.

THE 800 PILGRIMS, WITH FAITH AND HOPE, TRUSTED TO THE WISDOM AND THE COURAGE OF THE WHITE MEN.

AND JIM, ALONE IN HIS CABIN, FELT READY FOR ANY TEST. HE OFTEN READ A LETTER HE HAD RECEIVED FROM HIS FATHER.

"A SINGLE BAD ACT MAY BRING EVERLASTING RUIN ON A MAN. RESOLVE NEVER, THROUGH ANY POSSIBLE MOTIVES, TO DO ANYTHING WHICH YOU BELIEVE TO BE WRONG."

ONE NIGHT, AS JIM STOOD WATCH ON THE BRIDGE OF THE PATNA...

WHAT UNBOUNDED PEACE. HOW STEADY SHE GOES.

THE CAPTAIN CAME UP IN HIS PAJAMAS.

ALL IS WELL?

AYE, SIR.

THEN THE SECOND ENGINEER JOINED THEM.

HOT IS NO NAME FOR IT DOWN BELOW. T'AIN'T SAFE, EITHER. RUSTY PLATES, THIN AS BROWN PAPER, IS ALL THAT'S HOLDING THE SEA OUT.

SUDDENLY, THE SHIP GAVE A SHUDDERING LURCH.

WE'VE COLLIDED WITH SOMETHING.

GO FORWARD AND SEE IF THERE'S ANY DAMAGE. AND DON'T MAKE ANY NOISE OR YOU'LL CREATE A PANIC.

*J*IM RAN TO THE FOREPEAK HATCH.

IT'S HALF FULL OF WATER ALREADY. THERE MUST BE A BIG HOLE BELOW THE WATER LINE!

*W*HEN JIM REPORTED THIS TO THE CAPTAIN . . .

THE BULKHEAD WILL GIVE WAY ANY MINUTE. WE'LL GO DOWN LIKE A LUMP OF LEAD.

STOP MAKING SUCH A ROW! GO DOWN AND STOP THE ENGINES.

*T*HEN THE CAPTAIN SENT JIM DOWN TO CHECK THE BULKHEAD. IT WAS SO ROTTEN THAT FLAKES OF RUST FELL FROM IT.

*O*N HIS WAY BACK TO THE BRIDGE, JIM WALKED AMONG THE SLEEPING NATIVES.

NOTHING CAN SAVE THEM. THERE ARE 800 PEOPLE AND WE HAVE ONLY SEVEN BOATS-- AND NO TIME.

NO USE WAKING THEM. THERE WOULD JUST BE PANIC AND SCREAMS. I WOULD PREFER TO DIE QUIETLY.

ON THE BRIDGE, JIM FOUND THE CAPTAIN AND THE ENGINEERS TRYING TO LOWER A BOAT.

LEND A HAND, QUICK!

WHAT ARE YOU GOING TO DO?

WE'RE GOING TO CLEAR OUT. LET THE NATIVES GO DOWN WITH THE SHIP.

JIM DIDN'T SPEAK. HE DIDN'T MOVE.

ALL OF THESE PEOPLE TRUST THEIR LIVES TO ME. THERE IS NOTHING I CAN DO BUT SINK WITH THEM.

THE BOAT JAMMED.

COME AND HELP! DON'T YOU WANT TO SAVE YOUR OWN LIFE?

BUT JIM SPOKE ONLY TO THE SHIP.

SINK, CURSE YOU! SINK! GET IT OVER WITH!

ARE YOU MAD TO THROW YOUR ONLY CHANCE AWAY? LOOK THERE!

*H*E SAW A BLACK SQUALL WHICH HAD COME UP.

EVEN IF THIS ROTTEN HULK COULD FLOAT, THAT SQUALL WILL MAKE AN END OF HER FOR SURE!

*T*HE FRANTIC MEN FINALLY GOT THE BOAT CLEAR, BUT JIM KEPT HIS DISTANCE.

*T*HE BOAT DROPPED INTO THE WATER. THEN THE CAPTAIN AND TWO ENGINEERS REALIZED THAT THE THIRD ENGINEER WAS NOT WITH THEM.

WAIT! WHERE'S GEORGE?

GEORGE! JUMP! JUMP!

*B*UT GEORGE COULD NOT HEAR THEM. THE EXCITEMENT HAD STOPPED HIS HEART. HE WAS DEAD.

JIM, STANDING THERE WAITING TO DIE, COULD HEAR THEM CALLING TO GEORGE.

THERE ARE 800 LIVING PEOPLE ON THIS SHIP AND THEY'RE YELLING AFTER ONE DEAD MAN TO COME DOWN AND BE SAVED!

THEN THE SQUALL HIT.

THE SHIP BEGAN A SLOW PLUNGE; THE RAIN SWEPT OVER HER LIKE A BROKEN SEA.

JIM FELT SHE WAS GOING DOWN, DOWN, HEAD FIRST UNDER HIM.

GEORGE! JUMP! JUMP!

THEN--JIM JUMPED.

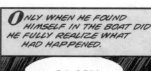

ONLY WHEN HE FOUND HIMSELF IN THE BOAT DID HE FULLY REALIZE WHAT HAD HAPPENED.

OH, GOD! WHAT HAVE I DONE?

I HAVE TUMBLED FROM A HEIGHT I CAN NEVER SCALE AGAIN. I WISH I COULD GO BACK! I WISH I WERE DEAD!

THE MEN IN THE BOAT SAW THAT IT WASN'T GEORGE.

WHY, IT'S THAT BLASTED MATE!

YOU WERE TOO MUCH OF A HERO TO LEND A HAND WITH THE BOAT, BUT HERE YOU ARE. WHY, YOU'RE NOT FIT TO LIVE.

WHEN THE SQUALL PASSED, THEY LOOKED FOR THE PATNA.

NOT A SIGN OF HER. SHE'S GONE DOWN.

NOBODY COULD HAVE HELPED HER. WE ESCAPED JUST IN TIME.

THE NEXT DAY, THEY WERE RESCUED BY A STEAMER. THE CAPTAIN GAVE THEIR STORY.

. . . WE TOOK MEASURES TO GET THE BOATS OUT WITHOUT CREATING A PANIC. AS THE FIRST BOAT WAS LOWERED, THE SHIP WENT DOWN IN A SQUALL. SHE SANK LIKE LEAD.

BUT SOME DAYS LATER, WHEN THEY REACHED PORT, THEY HEARD WHAT HAD REALLY HAPPENED. THE CAPTAIN HEARD IT FIRST.

THE *PATNA* DID NOT SINK. SHE WAS FOUND AFLOAT AND ABANDONED, BUT ALL OF THE PASSENGERS WERE SAFE. A FRENCH GUNBOAT TOWED HER TO PORT.

IT CANNOT BE! SHE SANK! SHE HAD TO SINK!

JIM GOT THE STORY LATER.

THERE WILL BE AN INVESTIGATION BY THE MARINE OFFICE. ARRANGEMENTS HAVE BEEN MADE FOR YOUR BOARD AND LODGING AT THE SAILOR'S HOME HERE.

BY THE TIME THE INVESTIGATION WAS HELD, THE CAPTAIN HAD FLED AND THE ENGINEERS WERE IN A HOSPITAL. ONLY JIM WAS THERE TO FACE IT OUT.

THE OFFICERS OF THE *PATNA* ARE CHARGED WITH ABANDONING, IN THE MOMENT OF DANGER, THE LIVES AND PROPERTY CONFIDED TO THEIR CHARGE.

JIM DENIED NOTHING, AND THE INVESTIGATION SOON CAME TO A CLOSE.

THE OFFICERS OF THE *PATNA* ACTED IN COWARDICE AND UTTER DISREGARD OF DUTY. SAILING CERTIFICATES OF ALL CONCERNED ARE HEREBY CANCELLED.

AS JIM AND THE SPECTATORS LEFT THE COURTROOM...

LOOK AT THAT WRETCHED CUR.

JIM SPUN AROUND.

DID YOU SPEAK OF ME?

NO, I DID NOT.

YOU SAY YOU DIDN'T, BUT I HEARD YOU. SINCE YOU SEE I'M NOT AFRAID, YOU TRY TO CRAWL OUT OF IT. WHO'S A CUR NOW?

THEN THE MAN UNDERSTOOD.

DON'T BE A FOOL. IT WASN'T I WHO SPOKE. AND NO ONE MEANT YOU AT ALL.

HE POINTED AT THE DOG.

FORGIVE ME. IT MIGHT WELL HAVE BEEN AS I SUPPOSED.

WHY DON'T YOU COME DINE WITH ME THIS EVENING? MY NAME'S MARLOW. I'M AT THE MALABAR HOUSE.

THAT EVENING AT DINNER, A LITTLE WINE OPENED JIM'S HEART AND LOOSENED HIS TONGUE.

I WOULD LIKE SOMEBODY TO UNDERSTAND--SOMEBODY--ONE PERSON AT LEAST. WHY NOT YOU?

EVER SINCE I WAS A LITTLE CHAP, I'VE DREAMED OF BEING ABLE TO MEET ANY EMERGENCY, ANY ADVENTURE. IT'S ALL IN BEING READY, I KNOW, YET I WASN'T. NOT--NOT THEN.

WHAT A CHANCE MISSED! MY GOD! WHAT A CHANCE MISSED!

DO YOU THINK I WAS AFRAID OF DEATH? I SWEAR I WAS NOT! WHEN I STOOD THERE ON THE BRIDGE, I WANTED IT TO SINK! I WANTED IT OVER!

I COULDN'T CLEAR OUT LIKE THE OTHERS.

BUT YOU DID--
AT THE LAST.

WHAT WOULD YOU HAVE
DONE? YOU ARE SURE OF
YOURSELF, AREN'T YOU?

BUT PUT YOURSELF IN
MY POSITION BEFORE
YOU ANSWER.

*THEY TALKED FOR QUITE
A WHILE. THEN*

AND NOW
WHAT WILL
YOU DO?
YOUR
CERTIFICATE
IS GONE...

HANG THE
CERTIFICATE!
I JUMPED,
DIDN'T I?
THAT'S WHAT
I HAVE TO
LIVE DOWN.

THE PROPER THING NOW
IS TO FACE IT OUT--
WAIT FOR ANOTHER
CHANCE TO PROVE
MYSELF.

THE FOLLOWING NIGHT, MARLOW SAW JIM AGAIN. HE GAVE HIM A LETTER.

I HAVE WRITTEN TO A FRIEND WHO OWNS A RICE MILL SOME DISTANCE FROM HERE. I HAVE ASKED HIM TO GIVE YOU A JOB. I HAVE SAID I CONSIDER YOU HONEST--AND TRUSTWORTHY.

HOW NOBLE OF YOU!

JIM GOT ON SPLENDIDLY IN HIS NEW JOB. BUT MONTHS LATER, MARLOW RECEIVED A LETTER FROM HIM. HE HAD LEFT HIS JOB.

THE ONE CHANCE IN A HUNDRED HAD HAPPENED. THE SECOND ENGINEER OF THE PATNA HAD TURNED UP IN THE MILL WHERE JIM WAS EMPLOYED.

HERE WE ARE TOGETHER AGAIN. BETTER THAN THE OLD SHIP, AIN'T IT?

WHEN MARLOW FINISHED JIM'S LETTER . . .

HE'S RUNNING AWAY. BUT IT'S ONLY HIMSELF HE'S RUNNING AWAY FROM.

JIM GOT A NEW JOB IN A PORT 700 MILES FROM THE RICE MILL. HIS DUTY WAS TO BOARD SHIPS AS SOON AS THEY CAME IN SIGHT OF PORT, AND GET THEIR CAPTAINS TO PURCHASE SUPPLIES FROM THE FIRM THAT EMPLOYED HIM.

RIGHT THIS WAY, SIR. MR. EGSTROM WILL TAKE YOUR ORDER FOR ANYTHING YOU NEED.

THAT'S A BRIGHT LAD YOU HAVE THERE.

BEST WATER CLERK WE EVER HAD. DON'T THINK HE'D MIND GOING OUT TO SEA IN AN OLD SHOE TO NAB A SHIP'S TRADE FOR THE FIRM.

BUT ONE DAY, IN THE SHOP...

EVER HEAR ABOUT THE PATNA THING?

WHO HASN'T HEARD ABOUT THOSE MEN DESERTING IT?

SKUNKS! EVERYONE OF THEM! I'D DESPISE BEING IN THE SAME ROOM WITH ONE OF THEM.

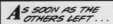

AS SOON AS THE OTHERS LEFT . . .

I'M LEAVING, SIR. I CAN'T WORK HERE ANY LONGER.

OHO! SO YOU WANT A RAISE! WELL, NAME YOUR FIGURE, JIM. ANYTHING WITHIN REASON.

IT ISN'T MONEY. IF YOU KNEW MY REASONS, YOU WOULDN'T WANT TO KEEP ME.

AND SO JIM LEFT. AS THE MONTHS PASSED, THERE WERE MANY OTHER EPISODES OF THIS SORT. SOMEONE WOULD LOOK SUSPICIOUSLY AT HIM-- OR SO HE WOULD THINK.

THE NEXT DAY, JIM WOULD BE ON HIS WAY TO A NEW PORT--WHERE SOMEONE, OR SOMETHING, WOULD CAUSE HIM TO MOVE ON AGAIN.

THAT REMINDS ME OF THE *PATNA* CASE.

JIM WAS ALWAYS ON THE MOVE. AND ALWAYS HE CARRIED WITHIN HIM A DOUBT OF HIS OWN COURAGE.

ONE DAY, HE MET MARLOW AGAIN.

YOU HAVE WASTED MANY OPPORTUNITIES.

BUT THEY HAVE MERELY BEEN OPPORTUNITIES TO EARN MY BREAD. I MUST HAVE SOMETHING ELSE-- AN OPPORTUNITY TO PROVE MYSELF.

*F*INALLY, MARLOW WENT TO SEE AN OLD FRIEND, STEIN, WHO OWNED MANY TRADING POSTS IN OUT OF THE WAY PLACES. HE TOLD HIM JIM'S STORY.

HE HAS TO GO SOMEWHERE WHERE HE CAN LEAVE HIS REPUTATION BEHIND HIM.

I COULD SEND HIM TO PATUSAN. IT IS A REMOTE DISTRICT OF A NATIVE STATE IN THE MALAY ARCHIPELAGO.

I HAVE A TRADING POST THERE, BUT THE AGENT IS A WORTHLESS FELLOW. JIM COULD REPLACE HIM, THOUGH I DON'T THINK HE WILL LEAVE THE PLACE. BUT HE CAN STAY, IF HE WANTS TO.

IT'S A DANGEROUS PLACE TO BE. RAJAH ALLANG, A THIEVING, MEAN LITTLE DESPOT, RULES AND ROBS THE COUNTRY-BORN MALAYS.

A HALF-BREED ARAB, SHERIF ALI, RULES THE INTERIOR TRIBES. ALI HAS A FORT ON A HILL ABOVE THE MAIN SETTLEMENT OF PATUSAN. FROM THERE, HE MAKES BLOODY RAIDS ON THE NATIVES.

ISN'T THERE ANYONE DECENT ON THE ISLAND?

YES, DORAMIN, THE CHIEF OF THE BUGIS. I MUST GIVE JIM THE RING DORAMIN ONCE GAVE ME FOR SAVING HIS LIFE. DORAMIN WILL DO HIS BEST FOR JIM.

YOUR JIM IS ROMANTIC. HE NEEDS A CHANCE TO LIVE HIS DREAMS OF GLORY. HE CAN DO IT IN PATUSAN

NOT LONG AFTER, JIM, WITH DORAMIN'S RING ON A STRING AROUND HIS NECK, WAS ON HIS WAY TO PATUSAN.

WHAT LUCK! WHAT A MAGNIFICENT CHANCE!

HE WAS PUT ASHORE AT A FISHING VILLAGE NEAR THE MOUTH OF A RIVER THAT FLOWED INLAND TO PATUSAN'S MAIN SETTLEMENT. FOR MOST OF THE NATIVES, HE WAS THE FIRST WHITE MAN THEY HAD EVER SEEN.

AT FIRST, THE NATIVES REFUSED TO TAKE JIM INLAND. THEY WERE AFRAID OF WHAT RAJAH ALLANG WOULD DO TO THEM IF THEY BROUGHT IN THIS WHITE STRANGER.

HANG THE RAJAH! I'M GOING INLAND, I TELL YOU!

THE ANGER OF THIS STRANGE MAN SEEMED SO GREAT THAT AT LAST A DUGOUT WAS GOTTEN READY AND PUT OFF.

FOR AMUSEMENT ON THE SLOW JOURNEY INLAND, JIM TRIED TO GUESS WHETHER THE OBJECTS HE SAW WERE FLOATING LOSS OR ALLIGATORS, BUT AFTER A DOZEN GUESSES...

THE FUN'S OUT OF THE GAME. IT'S ALWAYS AN ALLIGATOR.

FOR A WHILE, JIM DOZED. WHEN HE AWOKE, THE DUGOUT WAS COMING TO A BANK.

HIS THREE BOATMEN LEAPED OUT AND RAN. BUT BEFORE HE COULD RUN WITH THEM, RAJAH ALLANG'S MEN SURROUNDED HIM.

WHAT IS THIS? WHAT IS THE MATTER?

THE RAJAH WISHES TO SEE YOU.

JIM WAS MADE A PRISONER.

*F*OR THREE DAYS, JIM WAS THE RAJAH'S PRISONER, WHILE THE NATIVES TRIED TO DECIDE WHAT TO DO WITH HIM.

WHY HAS THE WHITE MAN COME? I AM MASTER HERE!

RAJAH, WOULD IT NOT BE BEST TO KILL HIM?

*T*HEN THEY ASKED HIM QUESTIONS.

THE RAJAH WISHES TO KNOW WHY THE WHITE MAN CAME TO THIS MISERABLE COUNTRY.

WOULD THE WHITE MAN LIKE TO GO BACK DOWN THE RIVER?

*J*IM FELT HIS POSITION WAS INTOLERABLE WITH A RUNNING START, HE MADE A LEAP FOR FREEDOM.

He LANDED ON THE OTHER SIDE WITH A FALL THAT JARRED HIS BONES.

He HEARD A GREAT YELL FROM THE STOCKADE AS HE RACED TOWARD A CREEK.

He TRIED TO LEAP ACROSS THE CREEK, BUT HE FELL SHORT, AND LANDED IN A SOFT AND STICKY MUDBANK.

With A TREMENDOUS EFFORT, HE TORE HIMSELF FROM THE SLIME.

Then HE RAN FOR THE SETTLEMENT HE SAW BEFORE HIM.

HE RAN INTO THE ARMS OF SEVERAL STARTLED NATIVES.

DORAMIN! TAKE ME TO DORAMIN!

HE WAS HALF-CARRIED, HALF-LED TO DORAMIN. HE GAVE THE CHIEF THE RING.

IT IS THE RING I GAVE MY TRUSTED FRIEND STEIN. YOU ARE WELCOME HERE.

THEN JIM COLLAPSED.

DORAMIN'S WIFE CARED FOR JIM AS THOUGH HE HAD BEEN HER OWN SON.

WHEN JIM WAS WELL AGAIN, HE MET DORAMIN'S ONLY SON, DAIN WARIS. DAIN WARIS BECAME THE BEST FRIEND JIM EVER HAD.

JIM DID NOT STAY WITH DORAMIN. HE FELT IT HIS DUTY TO LOOK AFTER STEIN'S BUSINESS, SO HE WENT TO LIVE WITH STEIN'S AGENT, CORNELIUS.

YOU CAN STAY HERE BUT IT WILL COST YOU TEN DOLLARS A WEEK. I DON'T MEAN TO KEEP YOU FOR NOTHING.

WHEN JIM TRIED TO CHECK STEIN'S BOOKS, HE FOUND THEM TORN OR MISSING.

ALL MY LATE WIFE'S FAULT. SHE MADE A TERRIBLE MESS OF THEM.

JIM INSPECTED THE STOREROOM.

WHERE ARE THE TRADE GOODS?

WHO CAN TELL? THE NATIVES ARE THIEVES --ALL OF THEM.

AND STEIN, TOO. YOU KNOW, HE OWES ME MONEY ON THE LAST THREE YEARS' TRADING.

WHAT A LOATHSOME LIAR!

CORNELIUS HAD A STEPDAUGHTER. HE ABUSED HER TERRIBLY. ONE DAY...

CALL ME FATHER-- AND WITH RESPECT. I AM A RESPECTABLE MAN!

WHEN CORNELIUS LEFT...

I CAN STOP HIM. JUST SAY THE WORD.

NO, HE IS UNHAPPY, TOO. IF I DID NOT FEEL SORRY FOR HIM, I WOULD KILL HIM WITH MY OWN HANDS.

I CAN DO NO GOOD FOR STEIN BY STAYING HERE. BUT I CANNOT DESERT THAT GIRL.

WHILE JIM STAYED WITH CORNELIUS, DORAMIN COULD DO NOTHING TO PROTECT HIM. BOTH RAJAH ALLANG AND SHERIF ALI, THE HALF-BREED ARAB WHO RAIDED PATUSAN REGULARLY, FELT JIM A THREAT. ONE NIGHT...

IF YOU CARE A PIN FOR YOUR LIFE, YOU'D BETTER GET OUT OF HERE. FOR EIGHTY DOLLARS, I'LL HAVE A MAN SMUGGLE YOU DOWN THE RIVER, ALL SAFE.

AFTER ALL, WHAT'S EIGHTY DOLLARS? A MERE TRIFLE--WHILE I'M COURTING DEATH BY GIVING YOU THIS CHANCE.

NO, THANKS. I DON'T INTEND TO LEAVE. I AM GOING TO LIVE HERE, IN PATUSAN.

YOU ARE GOING TO DIE HERE, IN PATUSAN.

GET UP! GET UP! GET UP!

HERE IS A REVOLVER. FOUR OF SHERIF ALI'S MEN ARE IN THE STOREROOM WAITING FOR THE SIGNAL THAT YOU ARE ASLEEP. THEY WERE GOING TO KILL YOU.

WHO WAS GOING TO GIVE THE SIGNAL?

CORNELIUS. ONLY I WATCHED YOUR SLEEP, TOO.

YOU!

DO YOU THINK I WATCHED ON THIS NIGHT ONLY?

OH, FLY! FLY! GO TO DORAMIN! THINK OF TOMORROW NIGHT, OF THE NIGHT AFTER. CAN I ALWAYS BE WATCHING?

JIM WENT TO THE STOREHOUSE, WITH THE GIRL FOLLOWING.

WAIT! YOU WILL NEED LIGHT. I WILL HOLD THE TORCH THROUGH THE WINDOW. WAIT TILL YOU HEAR MY VOICE.

NOW!

JIM PUSHED OPEN THE DOOR.

ONE OF THE MEN LEAPED AT HIM. AT THE SAME INSTANT, JIM FIRED.

THE OTHER THREE GAVE IN MEEKLY. JIM HAD THEM LINK ARMS.

MARCH! STRAIGHT TO THE RIVER!

WHEN THEY GOT TO THE RIVER BANK...

JUMP!

TAKE MY GREETINGS TO SHERIF ALI--'TIL I COME MYSELF.

NOW I AM LEAVING THIS HOUSE. AND YOU WILL COME WITH ME.

AFTER JIM LEFT CORNELIUS'S HOUSE, HE THOUGHT OF A PLAN TO RID PATUSAN OF SHERIF ALI.

HE HANGS OVER US LIKE A HAWK OVER A POULTRY-YARD. THE GODS THEMSELVES COULD NOT DESTROY HIM THERE.

BUT IF YOU DO AS I SAY, WE WILL DESTROY HIM.

DORAMIN AND DAIN WARIS AGREED TO JIM'S PLAN. AT NIGHT, JIM ORDERED THE NATIVES TO DRAG CANNON BELONGING TO DORAMIN UP THE HILL OPPOSITE SHERIF ALI'S CAMP.

WHEN THE CANNON WERE IN PLACE...

A FEW OF YOU WILL STAY HERE TO MAN THEM. THE REST OF US WILL STORM THE FORT.

BELOW THE FORT, THEY LAY IN THE WET GRASS, WAITING FOR DAWN.

WITH THE FIRST SLANT OF THE SUN'S RAYS, THE CANNON OPENED FIRE.

THE CANNON SHOT SPLINTERED THE WALLS OF THE FORT. THEN JIM AND DAIN WARIS LED THE CHARGE.

THEY WERE THE FIRST INSIDE THE SHATTERED FORT.

IN FIVE MINUTES, THE ROUT WAS COMPLETE. SHERIF ALI FLED THE COUNTRY.

WITH THE SMASHING OF SHERIF ALI, JIM BECAME THE VIRTUAL RULER OF PATUSAN. THE PEOPLE CALLED HIM TUAN JIM--LORD JIM--AND CONSIDERED HIM SOMETHING OF A GOD.

TUAN JIM DID BUT TOUCH WITH HIS FINGERS THE WALLS OF SHERIF ALI'S FORT--AND BEHOLD! DOWN THEY CAME!

IT IS WELL KNOWN THAT WHEN TUAN JIM FIRST CAME TO PATUSAN, THE TIDE TURNED TWO HOURS EARLY TO HELP HIM ON HIS JOURNEY.

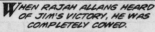

WHEN RAJAH ALLANG HEARD OF JIM'S VICTORY, HE WAS COMPLETELY COWED.

WE WILL DO AS TUAN JIM WISHES. WHO COULD RESIST AN ATTACK LED BY SUCH A DEVIL?

THE NATIVES TRUSTED JIM IMPLICITLY. HIS WORD DECIDED EVERYTHING.

YOU WILL GIVE BACK THE THREE BRASS POTS TO YOUR UNCLE. IT IS ONLY RIGHT.

TUAN JIM HAS SPOKEN WISELY.

JIM HAD A HOUSE BUILT IN PATUSAN. HE WAS HAPPY.

YOU WILL NEVER LEAVE ME, WILL YOU?

LEAVE YOU? LEAVE PATUSAN? NEVER! THIS IS WHERE I BELONG. I AM NEEDED HERE. HERE, I AM-- TRUSTED.

LOOK, MY JEWEL. THOSE PEOPLE SLEEP PEACEFULLY BECAUSE THEY BELIEVE IN ME. THERE IS NOT ONE HOUSE HERE IN WHICH I AM NOT TRUSTED.

IF YOU ASK THEM WHO IS BRAVE, WHO IS TRUE, WHO IS JUST, WHO IS IT THEY WOULD TRUST WITH THEIR LIVES, WHAT WOULD THEY SAY?

TUAN JIM.

THAT IS WHAT I WANT. THAT IS WHAT I MUST HAVE. THAT IS WHY I WILL NEVER LEAVE PATUSAN.

THEN ONE DAY A HUNGRY, BEATEN PIRATE NAMED BROWN CAME TO PATUSAN IN A STOLEN SHIP MANNED BY THIEVES AND CUTTHROATS.

WE NEED PROVISIONS AND HERE'S THE PLACE TO STEAL THEM. THE NATIVES WILL BE DEFENSELESS. MAYBE WE CAN GET SOME MONEY, TOO.

THE LONGBOAT WAS LOWERED AND THE PIRATES, LEAVING TWO MEN TO GUARD THE SHIP, SAILED UP THE RIVER. AS THEY NEARED THE PATUSAN SETTLEMENT...

SHOOT THE FIRST NATIVE YOU SEE. THEN WE'LL BURN A FEW HOUSES. THAT WILL PUT THE PROPER FEAR IN THEM.

BUT THE FISHING VILLAGE AT THE MOUTH OF THE RIVER HAD SENT A WARNING. SUDDENLY...

AMBUSH!

BROWN SPIED A NARROW CREEK THAT FLOWED INTO THE RIVER.

I'M HEADING THAT WAY. WE'VE GOT TO GET OUT OF THIS FIRE!

BROWN STEERED THE LONGBOAT INTO THE CREEK.

THAT KNOLL! WE CAN MAKE A STAND THERE!

THEY ABANDONED THE BOAT AND ESTABLISHED THEMSELVES ON THE HILL.

BROWN SET HIS MEN TO WORK BUILDING A BREASTWORK. HE EXPECTED THE NATIVES TO STORM THE HILL, BUT NO ONE APPROACHED.

WHAT ARE THE BEGGARS WAITING FOR?

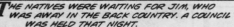

THE NATIVES WERE WAITING FOR JIM, WHO WAS AWAY IN THE BACK COUNTRY. A COUNCIL WAS HELD THAT NIGHT.

WE WILL NOT STORM THE HILL UNTIL TUAN JIM RETURNS.

I WILL TAKE SOME MEN TEN MILES BELOW THE SETTLEMENT. WE WILL BE ABLE TO CUT OFF THE EVIL ONES SHOULD THEY ATTEMPT TO ESCAPE.

MEANWHILE, BROWN, WAITING LIKE A HUNTED WILD BEAST AT THE TOP OF THE HILL, HEARD A VOICE CRYING--IN ENGLISH-- FOR PERMISSION TO ENTER THE BREASTWORK.

COME ON, THEN.

IT WAS CORNELIUS, FULL OF MORE HATE FOR JIM THAN HE COULD HOLD.

CORNELIUS TOLD BROWN ALL ABOUT JIM AND PATUSAN.

ALL YOU HAVE TO DO IS KILL JIM, AND THEN YOU'LL BE KING HERE.

JIM WILL COME HERE, WHEN HE RETURNS, AND ORDER YOU TO LEAVE HIS PEOPLE ALONE. EVERYBODY MUST LEAVE HIS PEOPLE ALONE. HE IS JUST LIKE A LITTLE CHILD.

BUT WHEN HE COMES HERE--JUST YOU KILL HIM STRAIGHT. THEN YOU CAN DO ANYTHING YOU WANT WITH HIS PEOPLE.

WHAT A MEAN LITTLE SKUNK THIS BEGGAR IS!

WHEN JIM RETURNED TO THE VILLAGE, THE NATIVES TOLD HIM ABOUT BROWN. HE MET THE PIRATE AT THE FOOT OF THE HILL.

WHAT MADE YOU COME HERE?

HUNGER. WHAT MADE YOU COME HERE?

JIM DID NOT ANSWER. THEN...

YOU'VE GOT US HERE LIKE RATS IN A TRAP, BUT EVEN A TRAPPED RAT CAN BITE.

WE DON'T ASK YOU FOR ANYTHING BUT TO GIVE US A FIGHT, OR A CLEAR ROAD TO GO BACK WHERE WE CAME FROM.

IF I LET YOU CLEAR OUT, WILL YOU SURRENDER YOUR ARMS?

SURRENDER OUR ARMS! YOU THINK I'VE GONE CRAZY? THAT AND THE RAGS I STAND IN IS ALL I HAVE GOT IN THE WORLD.

VERY WELL. I WILL TALK TO MY PEOPLE. YOU SHALL HAVE A CLEAR ROAD OR ELSE A CLEAR FIGHT.

JIM MET WITH THE NATIVES. IT WAS THEIR WISH TO FIGHT AND DESTROY THE PIRATES.

I DO NOT AGREE WITH YOU. YOU KNOW I HAVE NO THOUGHT BUT FOR THE PEOPLE'S GOOD. I HAVE NEVER DECEIVED YOU. I BELIEVE IT WOULD BE BEST TO LET THESE MEN GO WITH THEIR LIVES.

IF ANY HARM COMES TO YOU BECAUSE OF THIS, I WILL ANSWER WITH MY LIFE.

LORD JIM HAD SPOKEN, AND THE NATIVES BELIEVED HIM.

IT SHALL BE AS TUAN JIM SAYS.

LATER...

YOU ARE TIRED. WHERE ARE YOU GOING?

I AM GOING INTO THE TOWN. I AM RESPONSIBLE FOR EVERY LIFE IN THIS LAND.

ARE THE WHITE MEN VERY BAD?

MEN ACT BADLY SOMETIMES WITHOUT BEING MUCH WORSE THAN OTHERS.

JIM SENT HIS SERVANT, TAMB' ITAM, DOWN THE RIVER TO DAIN WARIS' CAMP.

TELL DAIN WARIS TO LET THE WHITE MEN PASS UNHARMED.

AND JIM SENT CORNELIUS TO TELL BROWN THAT HE WAS TO LEAVE AT DAWN.

YOU DIDN'T KILL JIM WHEN I TOLD YOU, AND WHAT DO YOU GET FOR IT? YOU ARE BETRAYED.

CORNELIUS TOLD BROWN ABOUT DAIN WARIS' ARMED PARTY WAITING DOWN THE RIVER.

BUT I KNOW ANOTHER WAY OUT OF THE RIVER. IN ONE PLACE IT PASSES BEHIND DAIN WARIS' CAMP.

BROWN DID NOT BELIEVE JIM INTENDED TREACHERY. BUT HE HATED THE WORLD, AND HE WANTED REVENGE. TWO HOURS BEFORE DAWN, CORNELIUS LED BROWN AND HIS MEN DOWN THE RIVER BEHIND DAIN WARIS' CAMP.

LOAD YOUR GUNS NOW. WE'RE GOING TO HAVE A CHANCE TO GET EVEN WITH THEM BEFORE WE'RE GONE.

IT WILL BE AS TUAN JIM WISHES. THEY SHALL PASS WITHOUT HARM.

LET THEM HAVE IT!

AIM LOW! AIM LOW!

AT THE SOUND OF THE FIRST SHOTS, DAIN WARIS RAN OUT UPON THE OPEN SHORE. HE RECEIVED A BULLET IN THE FOREHEAD, AND FELL LIFELESS TO THE GROUND.

BROWN'S MEN RETURNED TO THEIR BOAT AND FLED TO THEIR WAITING SHIP. BUT CORNELIUS WAS LEFT BEHIND. JIM'S SERVANT SAW HIM TRYING TO RUN AWAY.

NOW IT WAS PLAIN HOW THE PIRATES HAD LEARNED ABOUT THE BACK CHANNEL.

GET AWAY FROM ME! NO!

TAMB' ITAM STRUCK TWICE. THEN HE WATCHED WHILE CORNELIUS DIED.

THEN THE SERVANT RETURNED TO THE TOWN. HE WAS THE FIRST TO TELL JIM THE NEWS.

TUAN! THEY HAVE KILLED DAIN WARIS AND MANY MORE!

WHEN JIM HEARD THE STORY . . .

TAKE A MESSAGE TO DORAMIN! WE MUST ASSEMBLE BOATS FOR IMMEDIATE PURSUIT!

BUT THE SERVANT DID NOT LEAVE.

FORGIVE ME, TUAN. BUT IT IS NOT SAFE FOR THY SERVANT TO GO OUT AMONGST THE PEOPLE.

THERE IS MUCH WEEPING. MUCH ANGER, TOO.

THEN JIM UNDERSTOOD. HE WHO HAD BEEN ONCE UNFAITHFUL TO HIS TRUST HAD AGAIN LOST ALL MEN'S CONFIDENCE.

IT IS THE TIME TO FINISH. I SHALL GO TO DORAMIN.

NO! WE HAVE GUNPOWDER! RIFLES! WE MUST FIGHT FOR OUR LIVES!

I HAVE NO LIFE.

THOU ART MINE! DON'T LEAVE ME! IF YOU WILL NOT FIGHT, THEN LET US FLEE!

I CANNOT FLEE-- NOT AGAIN. IF I RAN NOW, I WOULD NOT BE WORTH HAVING.

JIM LEFT WITHOUT LOOKING BACK.

WHEN THE NATIVES SAW JIM THEY BEGAN TO MURMUR, AND JIM HEARD THEM.

HE CAME. HE HAS TAKEN IT UPON HIS OWN HEAD.

YES UPON MY HEAD.

JIM STOOD BEFORE DORAMIN.

I AM COME IN SORROW. I AM COME READY AND UNARMED.

DORAMIN, FULL OF RAGE, ROSE.

JIM FACED HIM WITH A PROUD AND UNFLINCHING LOOK. WHO COULD TELL WHAT FORMS, WHAT VISIONS, WHAT FACES, WHAT FORGIVENESS HE COULD SEE.

AND JIM FELL FORWARD, DEAD.

THE END

LORD JIM
JOSEPH CONRAD

Danger on the high seas, undaunted courage, native uprisings, scurvy pirates, naturally good native sidekicks, wicked native rulers, bold adventurers far beyond the pale of civilization—and honor lost and regained—these were the fixtures of boys' fiction in the late 1800s, very much as they are today in movies like *Raiders of the Lost Ark* or *The Ghost and the Darkness*, or in many role-playing games. These were the kind of stories that fill the mind of Jim—one of Conrad's greatest characters—and ultimately drive him to his destiny. But unlike the heroes of the thousands of stories written to amuse boys in the same period, Jim lives on in part because his author was not merely telling a tale of high adventure, but questioning the difference between high adventure as it is imagined, and adventures as they really happen. What would happen to someone who tried to make the real world work like cheap adventure fiction? What is the relation between ideals and actions? What happens when one's idea of oneself is false, yet one must try to live up to it? Those are the questions Conrad pursues in this great novel.

The Author

Joseph Conrad, who many rank as one of the greatest English novelists and a master of English style, did not even begin to learn English until he was twenty-one years-old. He was born Józef Teodor Konrad Korzeniowski (pronounced corts-awnny-off-ski), in 1857, in Berdyczów. At one time Berdyczów had been part of Poland, but in the 1700s Poland vanished from the map as it was cut up between its more powerful neighbors, Russia, Prussia and Austria. In 1857, Berdyczów was firmly within Russia; even later, when Poland was re-formed after World War I, it remained Russian, and today it's in Ukraine. It was about as far east as Polish settlement had ever gone; nonetheless, it was a Polish city, and young Józef's father, Apollo Korzeniowski, was a proud Pole.

It is significant that he was always called "Konrad" by his family: the name means knight or warrior, and the intent was that the young Konrad would be a fighter for free Poland, as well as a literary and cultivated man. Apollo Korzeniowski had fought an unsuccessful revolution against the Russians in 1830, and in 1863, when

The Making of a Reactionary

In the late 1800s, a few European nations controlled almost all of what we now call the Third World, either indirectly, by supplying the force behind the native rulers, or directly as colonies. Conrad traveled from colony to colony, carrying freight, mail, and passengers between various small white settlements in Asia, Africa, South America, Australia, and the Pacific Islands. Although he saw a great deal of the countries his ship took him to, like other white people in the colonies, he spent almost all of his time with other white Europeans.

This had a profound effect on him. Conrad had long ago repudiated the radical politics of his parents; he believed that revolutionary programs and idealistic crusades led only to disaster (certainly this had been true for his own family!). As he traveled the seas—a respected ship's officer and eventually a captain—he identified strongly with the white Europeans who managed the trading companies, commanded the local police, and ran the colonies in general. These were tough, hard men who, though they maintained law and brought modern technology to the colonies, also ruled by military force and a brutal system of punishments.

By today's standards, Conrad was a racist. He believed that only white people could be trusted to successfully operate the railroads, telegraphs, factories and other modern machinery of his day, or to maintain law, civilization, and peace, and therefore that only Europeans were fit to govern Asia, Africa, and Latin America. Furthermore, he believed that they had to rule to a great extent by force.

He seemed to reserve his special scorn for white idealists—reformers, Christian missionaries, socialists and so forth—who wanted to end, or soften, the oppression of the colonies. As he pointed out frequently in his novels, they all depended, for the civilized, gentle, and peaceful existence from which they condemned colonial brutality, on exactly that brutality. The comfortable life that gave them time, education, and refinement with which to feel sympathy with the oppressed was only possible because the oppression made them rich enough. Whether or not the reformers cared to admit it, the refined white upper- and middle-class life of the European nations rested on brutal working conditions in the factories, and on cheap natural resources extracted at gunpoint from the colonies. Conrad despised the reformers because he felt that their idealism was a way of saying that they wanted the gentle, safe life of the upper classes without having to know that it was paid for in blood; he insisted on facing up to where the wealth and civilization of Europe was coming from, and because he thought that gentle, sheltered world was a good one, he favored maintaining it by violence.

onrad was just six years old, Apollo elped lead another revolt. This one lso failed and, as a result, Konrad's arents were arrested and sentenced to "internal exile"—sent to a city or dis- ict where, it was hoped, the revolution- ries would be unable to ontact friends and fellow- onspirators. During the ong imprisonment which d up to this exile, both of onrad's parents fell ill; as result, his mother died hen he was seven, and his ather when he was twelve. e moved to the household f his uncle.

In 1874, sixteen-year- ld Konrad Korzeniowski ft Poland forever. At first he moved to e seaport city of Marseilles, in France, upposedly to attend school and to ecome part of the community of Polish xiles there (and perhaps to avoid being rafted into the Russian army); actually, e seems to have already made up his ind that he wanted to be a sailor.

In Marseilles he lived on a small lowance his uncle gave him, and spent great deal of time with a French friend few years older than he: Baptistin olary. Solary had sailed to the South acific a few years before, and had any contacts with shipping companies d sea captains. In the four years he ent in Marseilles, Konrad was able to et enough work as a sailor to spend out a year and a half at sea on various ips, mostly trading between arseilles and the French colonies in e Caribbean.

When ashore Konrad led a fairly ild life in the café society of the time.

He seems to have been involved in a variety of Carlist conspiracies (the Carlists were ultra-conservative support- ers of Carlos, who had some claim to be the rightful king of Spain, and who tried to seize power there during a brief civil war in the early 1870s. Marseilles had been a major center for Spanish exiles to gather to plot on behalf of Carlos, and many of them settled there after losing the war in 1876). Young Konrad Korzeniowski was also doing a great deal of drinking and carousing, hanging around with painters and poets when he was not at sea; by his own account he also did a great deal of reading in French—and the 1870s were one of the great periods of French literature. In any case, he was constantly writing to his uncle Tadeusz Bobrowski for more money, and his uncle wrote back to him, both to send money and to ask young Konrad to be at least a little more frugal. He also wrote to other relatives to complain of Konrad's misbehavior, which is how we know what we do of it.

In late 1877, just after Konrad's twentieth birthday, the French police got around to noticing that Konrad was not legally able to work on a French ship, and prevented him from taking a job on a ship; this brought on a crisis for him. Desperate for money, he invested the money he had left in a smuggling oper- ation in Spain, and though at first he made a profit and he was able to avoid arrest, by the end of the year he had lost all of his remaining money. He visited American ships and tried to join the

Conrad and the "N-Word"

Conrad's white characters often refer to non-whites as "niggers." To some extent this is simply Conrad mirroring the way in which white men on ships and in the colonies spoke at the time he was there. But it also reflects Conrad's basic view of the world, his idea that technology and civilized behavior would always be for whites only (and perhaps the occasional person of color, like Dain Waris, who acted like a white man).

The British Empire use of "nigger," as Conrad portrays it here, is slightly different from the way the word is used by today's vulgar racist Americans. It refers, not just to black African descent, but to virtually all non-whites, including, in this book, Malays, Arabs and Indonesians).

While Conrad was racist even for his day, it's important to realize that he was not unusual. The casual assumption of racial superiority was psychologically necessary for the Europeans who created and maintained the colonial empires, and Conrad was one of them. Though the word is painful to intelligent modern readers, the ideas behind it—of white superiority and the reduced worth of people of color—are far more offensive than his accurate representation of the way white men of his day talked. It would be a good thing if no one talked like these characters—but it would be a better thing if no one thought like them.

American navy (at the time you did not need to be an American citizen, or even to speak English). He borrowed more money and attempted to make his fortune gambling at Monte Carlo, but lost even the borrowed money. Finally, in late February of 1878, he tried to shoot himself, but the bullet he fired into his chest missed his heart by a fraction of an inch and came out on the other side, having done only minor damage.

As soon as Konrad recovered, he joined the English ship *Mavis*; for the next twelve years he pursued a career as an officer in the English merchant fleet. He had many adventures and sailed to every continent except Antarctica. Eventually he became captain of a ship sailing in the trade between Southeast Asia and Australia.

Konrad's political outlook was probably shaped by his career as a ship's officer. Ships at the time ran on iron discipline; sailors had to obey their officers' every order. In those days before radio, satellite navigation, helicopter rescue, and all the things that make modern sea travel much safer, the only thing that preserved a ship was the skill and knowledge of its captain and his officers, and thus it was literally a matter of life and death for everyone, especially common sailors, to obey orders, do the job they were given no matter how hard it was, and pull together. It has been suggested by many critics that Konrad saw the smooth working of a ship at sea as a model for what all of society should be like.

During the last years of the 1880s, after having learned English, Konrad became more and more interested in a career as a writer, but at first his English wasn't good enough and his chances were too uncertain for him to retire from the sea. Hoping to make a fortune, he took on a high-pay, high-risk job: he contracted with the Belgian company, owned by King Leopold, that ran the colony of the Congo (now Zaire) to take a river steamer most of the way up the Congo River (now the Zaire River) in Africa. This mission was extremely dangerous, for the Congo was "unimproved" (no one had ever cleared out the sunken logs and rocks from it) and largely uncharted, and many of the tribes along the way had not yet been subdued and sometimes attacked boats passing by. This mission became the basis of his famous short novel *Heart of Darkness*. On that voyage, he fell ill with dysentery and a variety of tropical fevers, and never fully recovered. For the rest of his life he was troubled by recurrent illness.

He had finished more than half of his first novel, *Almayer's Folly*, on the Congo mission. While recovering from the first attack of his illness, he began to write more seriously, and continued to write after taking a job as first mate of the *Torrens*, a freight and passenger ship working mainly in Australian waters. In 1893, John Galsworthy, a soon-to-be-famous English writer, happened to take a trip on the *Torrens*, and a friendship sprang up between Konrad and Galsworthy. Galsworthy strongly encouraged Konrad in his writing.

The year 1894 was a turning point in Konrad's life. Stranded by bad luck and illness, he had taken a job as second mate of a French merchant ship (a long step down for a man who had been a captain for several years). He wound up stranded in the French port of Rouen

without a job or a ship; he became involved with Jessie George, whom he eventually married; and most importantly, he made contact with Edward Garnett, a "first reader" (the editor who looks at manuscripts that arrive in the mail) at an English publishing house. To Conrad's amazement, Garnett accepted *Almayer's Folly* for publication. Thinking English readers would prefer an English-sounding writer, Konrad Korzeniowski legally changed his name to the one we know him by today: Joseph Conrad.

Garnett and Galsworthy introduced Conrad to most of the important writers in English in the 1890s and 1900s. This was a time of great artistic ferment, when what people expected of the novel and how people thought fiction should be written were changing rapidly. Among Conrad's friends and acquaintances were such famous writers as Ford Madox Ford, H. G. Wells, Henry James, Arthur Symons, Paul Valéry, and W. B. Yeats. Thus, although Conrad was politically an extreme conservative, he was strongly identified with the avant garde—artists trying to make radically new kinds of art.

His first two books sold very few copies and were commercial failures, but his third novel, *The Nigger of the "Narcissus,"* was at least a success with the critics, and sold well enough for Conrad to make a full-time occupation of writing. Though as late as 1895 he was still thinking of finding work as a ship's officer, the voyage to Rouen was his last as a professional sailor. His marriage to Jessie was a happy one, although there were periodic financial crises—the life of a writer, then and now, often involves periods of time when it's impossible to pay bills!

Following *The Nigger of the "Narcissus,"* he had a string of modest commercial publishing successes, including such now-famous works as *Lord Jim*, *Heart of Darkness*, *The Secret Agent*, *Nostromo*, and *Under Western Eyes*, which brought him some fame and security. Finally, in 1913, he had a commercial best-seller, *Chance*, which at last made him financially secure. Sadly, financial comfort seemed to arrive just as his powers as an artist were waning. He was only to write one more important novel—*Victory*—before his death in 1924.

AFTER TWO YEARS OF TRAINING, JIM WENT TO SEA. HE MADE MANY VOYAGES, AND WHILE YET YOUNG, BECAME CHIEF MATE OF A FINE SHIP.

WHY DON'T YOU COME DINE WITH ME THIS EVENING? MY NAME'S MARLOW. I'M AT THE MALABAR HOUSE.

Characters

Jim: The young man introduced on both the first page of Conrad's novel and the first page of the CI adaptation, Jim is a romantic idealist. He thinks life should be made up of grand adventures, and that people should live up to a very high idea of conduct. Jim is a young Englishman, the son of a country parson. We never learn his last name.

Marlow: The CI edition introduces Marlow as some sort of businessman, and underplays his importance to the story: he helps Jim out after the *Patna* incident . In the novel, Marlow is

one of the most important characters: he's the one who pieces together the story of what happened to Jim and why, and it is he who looks after Jim's situation following the *Patna* disaster. His visit to Patusan is an important episode in the novel as well. Marlow is also an important character in two other Conrad stories: *Youth* and *Heart of Darkness*. He always appears as a storyteller, a retired sea captain thinking about the meaning of life, and unfolding a story to illustrate the difficulties and complexity of real-life situations.

The Captain of the *Patna*:
An immensely fat, crude, and gross man, somewhere on the far side of middle age. (See following page.) Conrad calls him a "New South Wales German" (that is, one of the Germans, typically from Prussia or other parts of eastern Germany, who settled in the southeast corner of Australia at a time when Australia was a British colony) and gives him a thick accent. He seems to be Conrad's model of a bad, irresponsible captain . Jim despises him at once. The captain is apparently the one who makes the decision to abandon ship and leave the pilgrims to drown. (We don't know, because Jim, through whose eyes we see the situation, is not present when the decision is made.)

Why The CI Edition is Not the Novel

Most of Conrad's novels have very ordinary plots—often plots of the kind that would have been very familiar to Jim, who was a great reader of cheap adventure fiction. At first glance the characters in them—sailors, captains, merchants, adventures and "natives"—are only what you would find in any other book. So why have these books lasted so much longer than conventional adventure stories and sea stories?

When you read a Conrad novel, if you're really getting what Conrad is after, you aren't reading to find out what happens next (and it doesn't really matter even if you already know). And you aren't necessarily reading to spend time with the characters. Rather, you're reading to answer questions like "What is it really like to be there when courage is suddenly called for?" "How does an unsuccessful but generous person feel, deep in his or her heart, about someone else's success?" "What does a person do, moment by moment and day by day, until they become a completely different person?"

In this sense, Conrad was one of the first really modern writers. He always writes with an *ironic consciousness*: he doesn't just pour the story out naively, but writes in a way that lets us stand back from the story and see how things happen, why things might be the way they are, how every person differs from his or her stereotype. So we read Conrad with a kind of double vision—analyzing and commenting on the story as we read it.

By the nature of its format and when it was published (1957), the CI adaptation can't do this. For example, a large part of the book is concerned with how Marlow came to hear of Jim's story, and how the story came to be important to Marlow. In the CI adaptation, Marlow is only there briefly, and we learn the story without any questioning of how the facts could have become available, and without many of the small, subordinate stories that throw light on the meaning of the novel. Or consider that in the book nearly every character, no matter how minor, has some quirks or traits to remind us that this person had a life before we saw them in the book, and often had a life afterward. The CI adaptation tends to reduce them to square-jawed heroes like Jim and Dain Waris, rascally non-whites like Rajah Allang and Sherif Ali, and low-browed hairy villains like the captain of the *Patna*, Brown, and Cornelius—that is, to the kind of character that would be in every adventure story.

Where Conrad writes the story to explore its meaning, the CI adaptation simply tells the story. But it isn't Conrad's story that makes *Lord Jim* a great book: it's the way he tells it.

The *Patna* Engineers:

The Chief: the man in charge overall of the *Patna's* main engines, of whom we know little except that he drinks on the job and he and Jim don't like each other.

The Second: who has a broken arm, drinks when he can, and is a lower-class person. Here you can see Conrad's reactionary views, for though the second engineer is credited with some courage and intelligence, it is made clear that it's a horrible burden for Jim to have to associate with someone so low-bred.

The Third, or the "Donkey Man": We are

GO FORWARD AND SEE IF THERE'S ANY DAMAGE. AND DON'T MAKE ANY NOISE OR YOU'LL CREATE A PANIC.

told his name is George. A "donkey" is an engine used when the main engines are shut down, thus a donkey man is one who operates the donkey when it's needed. Usually his duties are to assist the chief and second. He suffers a fatal heart attack that is an important part of the plot.

The Lascars: A "lascar" is a native sailor; one reason why the *Patna* survives (and the CI edition does not make this clear) is that when the European crew abandons her, none of them bother to talk to the lascars, and thus the helmsman and other crew remain at their duty stations. The lascars provide an important contrast to Jim: they don't know what is going on, but they do their duty, and in that regard they prove to be his moral superiors.

The French Lieutenant: This character doesn't appear in the CI edition, although dialogue does refer to a French gunboat that towed the *Patna* to port. This French naval officer was part of the party that boarded the *Patna* and set up a tow-line to pull the *Patna* to the nearest British-controlled port. Since the *Patna* could drag the gunboat to the bottom with her if she were to sink, it's necessary to have someone watching the hawser (the tow-rope) to cut it if the *Patna* starts to go down. As a point of honor, the French lieutenant elects to watch the hawser from the deck of the *Patna*, insuring that he will share the fate of the eight hundred pilgrims. For thirty hours he stands watch over the hawser, always waiting for the crash of the bulkhead giving way and the necessity of cutting the line. When Marlow later asks him if he can understand Jim's fear, the lieutenant says that, of course, the situation on the *Patna* was very frightening, but "what life may be worth when the honor is gone...I can offer no opinion, because, monsieur, I know nothing of it." In this way the lieutenant supplied another extremely important contrast to Jim: the lieutenant certainly had not contracted (as Jim had) to deliver the pilgrims to their destination, let alone to save their lives, and yet he does it. He refuses to understand Jim's situation: the lieutenant has kept his honor, and is in a different part of the human race than Jim, who has lost his.

Captain Brierly: He doesn't appear by name in the CI adaptation, but he's extremely important in the novel. He is one of the chief judges at Jim's trial—technically an Inquiry. An Inquiry is concerned with establishing the facts in a sea accident, and with deciding whether the ship's officers should be allowed to keep their licenses. Normally the judges at an Inquiry will be sea captains, because they have the expertise to evaluate the decisions made by the officers in the emergency. Because, as he investigates the accident, what he hears makes him call everything he has believed into question, Captain Brierly later commits suicide; too many things he thought certain have been shown to be completely unreliable. This is part of how Conrad reminds us that the question posed by Jim's offense is a very serious one; apparently Brierly can't live with that question open.

Marlow's Friend, the Rice-Mill Owner: This is the person to whom Marlow first writes to get Jim a job. In the novel itself, it's clear that this unnamed character becomes very fond of Jim and regards him as a son, and thus he's terribly hurt, losing all his faith in humanity, when Jim abruptly leaves work at the rice mill. The rice-mill owner does not know, of course, that Jim was chief mate of the *Patna*, or that the *Patna's* second engineer has come to work in his rice mill, reminding Jim of the incident.)

Engström and Blake : These two partners own a ship-chandler firm (a ship-chandler sells supplies for a ship); in the CI version we see only Engström. In Conrad's novel Blake and Engström are two contrasting physical and psychological types— Blake small, dark, and constantly picking on Engström, and Engström big, blond and quietly ignoring most of what Blake is saying. Engström, too, is dreadfully disappointed at Jim's sudden disappearance; this helps to set up the difficulty that Marlow, Brierly and Stein have when they discover that Jim is subtly, dangerously, not what he appears to be.

Stein: Marlow's old friend, the butterfly collector. In the book we learn that he originally came out to the islands as an assistant to a scientist, and after the scientist returned home, went to work for a trader in the area, eventually building up a substantial trading house.

I HAVE A TRADING POST THERE, BUT THE AGENT IS A WORTHLESS FELLOW. JIM COULD REPLACE HIM, THOUGH I DON'T THINK HE WILL LEAVE THE PLACE. BUT HE CAN STAY, IF HE WANTS TO.

Marlow turns to him to find employment for Jim somewhere where no one who knows of the *Patna* will ever come.

Tunku Allang: The rajah of Patusan. Rajahs are traditional political leaders, the equivalent of kings and dukes, in the Islamic parts of India and South Asia. Most of Conrad's readers would have associated a rajah with great wealth, so there's an ironic joke in Tunku Allang's "palace" being a log stockade with mud huts inside . Tunku Allang is the leader of one important faction in Patusan— he's the traditional leader of most of the people of the town.

Doramin: Doramin is an old friend of Stein's. We never find out how they became close friends, but Jim is carrying a ring from Stein that Doramin gave him as a pledge of faith many years before . Doramin is the father of Dain Waris, who is later Jim's best friend. He is also the leader of the Bugis people, who are a group of Malays who have come to Patusan to set up a trading camp. The Bugis are loyal to Doramin rather than to Tunku Allang, and form the second side of the three-way struggle going on in Patusan when Jim arrives.

Dain Waris: Doramin's oldest son, and Jim's best friend, war-comrade, and base of support in Patusan. Dain Waris is also about as close as Conrad ever gets to a favorable portrayal of a person of color—mainly by emphasizing repeatedly that Dain Waris thinks like a European.

Sherif Ali: A robber and pirate whose band forms the third side of the three-way struggle going on in Patusan when Jim arrives. His name is Ali; "Sherif" is an Islamic title implying aristocratic birth. It seems very unlikely that this bandit is actually of noble

descent. His band of robbers occupies one of the two high hills that looks down on Patusan, and has built a stockade there. This small fortress militarily dominates Patusan until Jim, and Dain Waris, find a way to destroy it.

Cornelius: Cornelius is Stein's old agent in Patusan, the person who had Jim's job before Jim got it. In the novel we learn that he was married to a Eurasian woman, with whom some scandal was connected. (It's suggested that Jewel had already been born by the time Cornelius married her mother, and that he's Jewel's stepfather, not her father.) Stein's sent the couple to Patusan, possibly to conceal the problem from public view; it was apparently Stein's idea that the woman would run the business, but after she died Cornelius took it over and has done a very poor job of running it ever since. Jim goes to Patusan with a letter from Stein, firing Cornelius and giving Jim his job.

Jewel: Cornelius's stepdaughter, the daughter of the mysterious Eurasian woman who was sent to Patusan decades before, and Jim's native "love." Conrad was very coy about just how sexual the relationship might be between Jim and Jewel, because white readers at the time might be offended by the possibility of sex between the races, but it's

clear from the context that both Jewel and Jim regard themselves as married. Jewel is not her real name, but it's the only name we learn; it's Jim's pet name for her.

Tamb'Itam: A physically strong, highly intelligent young Bugis who becomes Jim's loyal bodyguard. Silent, loyal, deadly in a fight, you could look on him as someone who embodies the virtues that Conrad thinks are vital in a follower. You could also see him as a very standard non-white sidekick—the cousin of the Lone Ranger's Tonto, the Green Hornet's Kato, or Huck Finn's Jim. In any case, Conrad puts much of the common-sense and pragmatic judgment of Jim into Tamb'Itam's mouth, for after Jim's death, Tamb'Itam conveys Jewel safely back to Stein, and provides

Marlow with most of the report we will ever get on what actually happened in Patusan.

Gentleman Brown: A pirate, well-known throughout the South Seas as "Gentleman" Brown; Conrad never tells us where he got the nickname. Brown is Conrad's model of the "bad white man" in that his only purpose is to plunder and despoil the people of Patusan (in fact he's astonished when he realizes that that is not what Jim has been doing, since that's the only reason he can imagine for going to a remote and backward area). He also clearly embodies the dangerous forces of envy, sheer spite, and cruelty that Conrad sees as always lurking just below the surface of civilization—it's Brown's decision to murder Dain Waris

What Was It Then and What Is It Now?

If you pull out a map to see where Conrad's characters are going, you may find that you can't locate many of the places he mentions. As colonial empires collapsed, places were renamed (or took back their own names) in the languages of the people who lived there. Here are a few place names that have changed since Conrad's time:

Then	*Now*
Batavia	Jakarta
Burma	Myanmar
French Indo-China	Vietnam, Cambodia, Laos
Malay Archipelago	Indonesia
Penang	Pahang
Saigon	Ho Chi Min City
Samarang	Samarinda
Siam	Thailand

and his Bugis followers during the pirates' retreat down river, not because it gains the escaping pirates any advantage, but simply because it will inflict harm. When Marlow meets the dying Brown, years later, the old pirate is overjoyed to learn that his spiteful action eventually cost Jim his life.

The question of "how Conrad tells it" is most significant when considering the plot of *Lord Jim*—as *opposed* to the narrative. What's the difference? A **narrative** is a connected series of events; the narrative that forms the background of Conrad's novel, and the foreground of the CI adaptation, is pretty similar:

Jim, an attractive and promising young officer in Britain's merchant marine, dreams of being a hero. A crisis arises in which Jim, instead of heroically standing by the passengers and the lascar sailors of the *Patna*, deserts with the other officers. (See previous page). Only Jim stays for the Inquiry—the others flee. Jim can no longer work as a ship's officer because the Inquiry "pulls his papers"—that is, revoked his license.

Marlow finds Jim a job, and then more jobs, because every time Jim's secret comes out, he flees further east (further from Europe, toward the Malay Archipelago, what is now called Indonesia). Finally Jim goes to the remote state of Patusan, where he finds many friends (especially Tamb'Itam and Dain Waris), a lover (a girl he calls Jewel), a sort of adopted family (Dain Waris's family, especially his father Doramin), and an important job (as *Tuan* Jim, for all practical purposes the local ruler). Thus he regains all that he had lost by his moment of cowardice.

The settlement is attacked by the pirate, Brown. Jim gives Brown safe conduct to leave, promising that the Bugis people (who wanted to attack Brown and kill, or take him prisoner) that if any Bugis is harmed, he will take full responsibility. Out of sheer meanness, Brown kills Dain Waris in a surprise attack. Though Tamb'Itam and Jewel beg him not to, Jim goes to Doramin to take responsibility for Dain Waris's death, and Doramin shoots him dead.

That's the way the CI adaptation tells the tale, and the captions tell us why Jim takes this or that action. But Conrad was after bigger game, asking bigger questions: why does anyone do anything? why does it matter what we do? does it matter why we do it?

The way in which an author arranges the events of the narrative, and the way and order in which the reader encounters them, is the **plot**. Where the CI adaptation untangles the events of Conrad's plot into a smooth line, Conrad vants to show the reader how even the implest things are difficult to learn bout, and hard to understand if we do earn about them— nd just might not add up to a meaning, no matter how much we earn.

In Conrad's *Lord Jim*, we watch Marlow ry to understand Jim's story. To understand it he must first piece it together from what Jim tells him at their several meetings and n his letters, plus what he happens to earn from others. In

that sense it's something like a detective story, except that the mystery isn't about who did it, or how, or why. Marlow, though he doesn't know when he starts down the trail of the mystery, is trying to find out *why it matters*.

How does Conrad unravel his story to us? For the first three chapters, we know that someone is telling us a story; it begins with Jim working for Engström and Blake— that is, we see him as a talented water-clerk, long after the *Patna* incident and Inquiry, and long before the incidents in Patusan. We learn that he was being pursued by a "fact" which "followed him casually but inevitably."

Suddenly we drop back to the story of how Jim went to sea, how he was trained, what jobs he held first, and how he happened to end up on the *Patna*. Then, at the beginning of Chapter 4, we leap forward to Jim, sitting on trial—but we don't know for what, just yet. Finally, at the beginning of Chapter 5, we find out that Marlow is telling the story to a group of old friends, and that Marlow attended Jim's trial out of curiosity, after happening to have seen Jim come in to port. Chapter 6 picks up the story of the trial—still not telling us what happened on the *Patna*—but also introduces the subplot of Marlow's old acquaintance Captain Brierly, who sits in judgment on Jim, asks Marlow to encourage Jim to run away before the trial is done, and who—a few months afterward, mysteriously commits suicide. In the same chapter, the incident of the yellow dog occurs (previous page illustration.) which leads to Marlow having dinner with Jim (mostly to satisfy his curiosity about the *Patna* incident, but also out of kindness to a friendless man).

In the rest of Chapter 7, and all the way through

finally learn of the *Patna* incident from Jim's viewpoint, as he tells his story to Marlow (and remember the reader is learning it because Marlow is repeating the story to the narrator of the book). But there is also a vast amount of argument between Marlow and Jim (because Marlow dislikes Jim's actions), and Marlow supplies us with a number of incidents from the trial and conversations he had with other people years afterward, to give us a sense of whether or not Jim is truthful. The added evidence makes the case even more difficult and confusing. But finally, in Chapter 9, we do learn about his jumping from the ship, and in Chapters 10-12 we learn about how the officers of the *Patna* took off in a lifeboat, leaving the pilgrims and lascars to their fate. In Chapter 12, continuing into Chapter 13, we also hear how Marlow, years later, happened to run into the French lieutenant who was in charge of towing the *Patna*, and thus Marlow confirms more of the complex difficulty of the story. At this point Marlow seems to be interested mainly because he had thought he was a good judge of people, and he would have trusted Jim—and Jim is not trustworthy.

We quickly come to see that Marlow is afraid that if he can't trust Jim he may not be able to trust himself. (Perhaps this question is what drives Brierly to suicide; it may be why the French lieutenant won't discuss the case beyond a certain point.) Chapter 14

brings us back to the trial, where Marlow meets a man named Chester, who has a business offer for Jim—a dreadful job on a guano island (an island where old bird dung is mined to make fertilizer). Chapters 15-17 tell how Marlow was interrupted many times but was finally able to meet with Jim and persuade him to take a job with the rice-mill owner (with Chapter 16 briefly flashing forward to Patusan); but this time Marlow himself isn't sure why he's helping Jim, or why he wants to know what becomes of him. Chapter 18 tells about Jim getting and losing many jobs as he works his way east—and now we are all the way back to where we began the story, with Jim the waterclerk pursued by a "fact."

In Chapters 19-23, we see Marlow enlist Stein's help: the two of them hit on the plan to send Jim to Patusan, where no one is ever apt to bring up the story of the *Patna*. But while all this is going on we also see a great deal more of Marlow's relationship with Jim, and we learn many stories about Stein and other characters. We also are reminded at times that Marlow is telling this tale to a still-unspecified narrator, who is reporting what he heard from Marlow. There's a great deal of complex trouble about Marlow trying to make sure Jim has both a pistol and the ammunition for it (Jim goes off without bullets at first)

Chapters 24 and 25 tell the story of Jim's arrival in Patusan, his capture

THE FOLLOWING NIGHT, MARLOW SAW JIM AGAIN. HE GAVE HIM A LETTER.

I HAVE WRITTEN TO A FRIEND WHO OWNS A RICE MILL SOME DISTANCE FROM HERE. I HAVE ASKED HIM TO GIVE YOU A JOB. I HAVE SAID I CONSIDER YOU HONEST--AND TRUSTWORTHY.

y Rajah Tunku Allang's men, and his scape to join Doramin's Bugis peole. As we hear the story we learn hat Marlow learned it by visiting 'atusan years later, and that Patusan pparently had changed completely rom what it had been when Jim rrived, so we are both hearing of deserate adventures (from Jim) and valking through the peaceful garden hat Jim has made of Patusan (with Marlow).

In Chapters 27-29 we learn how im and Dain Waris defeated Sherif Ali, how Jim fell in love with Jewel nd incurred Cornelius's hate—but we ear the different stories as Marlow icked them up, in seemingly random rder. Even though these things happened after Jewel saved Jim's life from herif Ali's men, we only hear of that ncident in Chapters 30-32, because 's the lead-up to a very important cene in Chapter 33, n which Jewel takes Marlow aside and sks him why Jim is iding so far out in 'atusan (this scene oes not appear in ne CI version). She sks because she's fraid Jim will leave er. When Marlow inally tells her the ruth—that Jim is ere because he did omething shameful nd can't bear to be een by his fellow white men—she efuses to believe him.

In Chapters 34 and 35, Marlow eems to be bringing Jim's story to a conclusion in which he has found some peace of mind and happiness as the *Tuan* of Patusan. But in Chapter 36, the narrator (who has been listening to Marlow all this time), years *after* hearing the story, receives a letter from Marlow about what finally happened to Jim. This is the story of Gentleman Brown, which continues through Chapter 45—with digressions in which Marlow explains how he met Tamb'Itam and Jewel at Stein's place, how the whole incident has severely depressed Stein, how it happened that Brown picked Patusan as a target, and how Marlow happened to meet Brown later, and thus got a vital part of the story from him.

Thus, the plot of Conrad's novel is not about "Jim and what happened to him," but about what Marlow, Stein, the nameless narrator, and others come to see as the *meaning* of the story of Jim; how Jim's story comes to matter profoundly. It's not what happens in the book (entertaining as the adventure is) but the way in which the people around Jim come to understand it, that makes Conrad's novel the great book it is. We open *Lord Jim* as if it were "light holiday reading" that starts Jim going to sea and on a series of adventures, but finish it wondering about the meaning of action, life, love, loyalty, and honor. The more we learn of what happened

The more we learn of what happened to Jim, the less we can be sure what it all means—except that we know that it matters very much, not just to Jim but to all of us.

One way Conrad enriches his story is with symbolism: using certain kinds of events and objects to enhance the mood or emphasize the importance of what is happening. In Chapter 1, we see Jim fail to get into a rescue boat quickly enough, and thus miss his first chance for heroics while still on the training ship. Later, of course, he gets into the boat from the *Patna* when he shouldn't (and misses his chance for adventure-book heroics again). Then he won't get onto a boat and avoid his trial. Then he *does* get into a boat to go to Patusan (where his honor will be revived), and finally he *won't* get onto a boat to save his life—his newly re-won honor is too important to him. And that doesn't begin to cover the number of times that people getting into or out of boats in this book is significant. Each incidence is flavored a little bit by all the previous incidents we've read of, and each adds its own special take on the basic situation of "getting into a boat to get away." The notion of sailing away is a common symbol, both for beginning a new life and for putting the past behind one; Jim seems to have trouble doing either.

Or consider how often we read the phrase "he was one of us." At first it seems clear what Marlow means—that Jim was a white sea-faring officer, like Marlow and other white officers, who looked like he could do his job. Or is Jim "one of them" because of his weaknesses?

But later Dain Waris—who is not European—is declared to be "one of us," and not long after that we see the other Bugis debating, unsure of whether Dain Waris can pull of the defense against Brown, because they're not sure who Waris is "one of."

For another kind of symbol, look at the many examples of courage and steadfastness held up in contrast to Jim. Marlow really learns of an amazing amount of genuine heroism as he investigates Jim's cowardice: the lascars (who didn't know what the situation was but kept doing what they were supposed to do), the French lieutenant (who understood the danger perfectly but faced it because his honor demanded it), Tamb'Itam (who can't understand that Brown has activated Jim's shame), Stein (who went into that country with nothing but a butterfly net), and many others.

Finally, a symbol doesn't have to be powerful. For example, it's Brierly who sees to the heart of the *Patna* officers' mistake, and knows he could have made himself. He figures out what actually happened to the *Patna* when it looked, to the deserting officers in the lifeboat, as if she must be sinking; she had actually come around to "put her bow to the sea" (aim into the oncoming waves—a safer and more stable position for a ship in a storm) so that at the moment they saw the light dip and appear to vanish, the *Patna*—without her officers—was actually moving into a much safer position. Where all intellectual ability had fled and the 'civilized' white leaders had abandoned the pilgrims to their doom, the old ship and the lascar sailors had already done what was needed.

Conrad the Pessimist

Conrad's political convictions disposed him to see the world as moving from bad to worse. He had great admiration and respect for the accomplishments of the Europeans of his day—the conquest of essentially the whole Earth, far-flung exploration, scientific discovery, astonishing technological advances, the bringing of law and order to areas that had known only banditry. But he felt strongly that all of these accomplishments were just a thin surface layer, and that underneath it all was the old barbarism, cruelty, and incompetence that the world had known since its dawn.

In light of this, consider Jim's career. Conrad makes it clear that although Jim had very high ideals, he got them from cheap and silly sources: the adventure stories he had read as a boy. Furthermore, in the novel Jim was on the *Patna* in part because he had learned to love the safety and comfort of sailing in the Indian Ocean, compared with the more difficult voyages in the North Atlantic that would have taken him closer to home. So it's hardly surprising that Jim discovers he can't live up to his own ideals. Indeed, none of the white officers of the *Patna* do; the lascars give a better account of themselves, but only because they're ignorant of the real situation.

Jim certainly "civilizes" Patusan, in that after his arrival it becomes a safer, better place to live; but Jim doesn't do that all by himself, and he does it under false pretenses. It's the people of Patusan, especially the Bugis tribe, who do the work, and most of them knew it needed doing already. It is their faith in Jim that lets them achieve this, but their faith is misplaced, for Jim can make mistakes like anyone human, and he has already badly betrayed one trust. Even though Gentleman Brown doesn't know of Jim's past, Jim still lives so much in shame and fear of what he has done that he becomes paralyzed, unable to mount any sort of defense. Progressive, "civilized" Patusan collapses right back into the misery in which he first found it, and the only real difference is that Jim is dead. So for all his emphasis on the importance of "white civilization," Conrad himself seems to have had little faith that it would be effective in the long run. While he seems to have thought of progress as a noble attempt, he expected it to fail. The question he puts before us is, "If progress and civilization fail, how do we then live?" And it would be fair to say that for many of his heroes, Jim among them, the answer is: we don't. We just hope to die gracefully.

• What is it about Jim that frightens Marlow, Brierly, the French lieutenant, and the other experienced seamen? Why aren't they similarly disturbed by the "New South Wales German" captain?

JIM FELT HIS POSITION WAS INTOLERABLE. WITH A RUNNING START, HE MADE A LEAP FOR FREEDOM.

• Jim is angry about having "missed his chance." If he had not—if he had stayed with the *Patna*—would he have been "satisfied," as Marlow uses the word at the end of the novel (and as Jim uses it earlier when the two of them are talking)?

• How is Tamb'Itam a standard non-white sidekick? Is he different in any important ways?

• Stein barely knows Jim, doesn't appear until quite late in the book, and is involved in only one major point of the plot; yet the last lines of Lord Jim (quoted from a letter from Marlow) are: "Stein has aged greatly of late. He feels it himself, and says often that he is 'preparing to leave all this; preparing to leave...' while he waves his hand sadly at his butterflies." Why is a "minor" character given such a prominent place?

• Why does Cornelius keep complaining that Jim is "like a little child?" Even if Jim is "like a little child," why should that bother Cornelius?

• The CI adaptation has Jim making his break over Allang's wall when the guards ask him questions. In the novel itself, Jim is sitting trying to repair an old clock for Allang when he suddenly realizes that if he doesn't escape he will probably be killed. What's the symbolism of the old clock? Why do you think it was omitted from the CI adaptation?

About the Essayist:

John Barnes is an Assistant Professor in the Communications Department at Western State College in Gunnison, Colorado. He holds a Ph.D. in Theater from the University of Pittsburgh. In addition, Mr. Barnes is the best-selling author of *A Million Open Doors*, *Mother of Storms*, and *Kaleidoscope Century*.